I0805373

Good Night, Bears

Learning About Hibernation

Emily Wilson

ROSEN COMMON CORE READERS

Rosen Classroom™

New York

Published in 2013 by The Rosen Publishing Group, Inc.
29 East 21st Street, New York, NY 10010

Book Design: Michael Harmon

Photo Credits: Cover Bruce M. Herman/Photo Researchers/Getty Images; p. 4 auremar/Shutterstock.com; p. 5 Daniel J. Cox/Oxford Scientific/Getty Images; p. 6 EPG_EuroPhotoGraphics/Shutterstock.com; pp. 7, 20 Evgeny Murtola/Shutterstock.com; p. 8 visceralimage/Shutterstock.com; p. 9 Tony Campbell/Shutterstock.com; p. 10 Igor Borodin/Shutterstock.com; p. 11 S. J. Krasemann/Peter Arnold/Getty Images; p. 12 Piotr Sikora/Shutterstock.com; pp. 13, 14 John Serrao/Photo Researchers/Getty Images; p. 15 Tim Rains/Shutterstock.com; p. 16 Jim Chagares/Shutterstock.com; p. 17 AllessandroZocc/Shutterstock.com; p. 18 Sven-Erik Arndt/Picture Press/Getty Images; p. 19 Ron van Elst/Shutterstock.com; p. 21 Brad Whitsitt/Shutterstock.com.

ISBN: 978-1-4488-8776-7
6-pack ISBN: 978-1-4488-8777-4

Manufactured in the United States of America

CPSIA Compliance Information: Batch #WS12RC: For further information contact Rosen Publishing, New York, New York at 1-800-237-9932.

Word Count: 176

Contents

Do you ever feel sleepy?
Do you go to bed?

Bears get sleepy, too.
They sleep for the whole winter.

Hibernation means that a bear sleeps for the whole winter.

Do you know how bears get ready
to sleep?
It takes a lot of work!

Bears look for food all summer.

Bears eat a lot!

Bears eat so they can get fat.

Extra fat lets bears sleep
for the whole winter.

Bears sleep in a den.

Dens can be in logs or caves.

Dens are warm.

They keep bears safe.

Bears like sleeping on beds.
They use leaves, sticks, and grass.

The bears lay on their beds.
They go into a very deep sleep.

Sometimes, baby bears are born in the winter.

Baby bears are called cubs.
Their mom keeps them warm in the den.

Cubs grow every day.
They even grow while they sleep!

The bears are hungry when they wake up.

The bears go outside to hunt and play.

Next winter, the bears will
hibernate again.

Do you know any other animals that hibernate?

How a Bear Hibernates

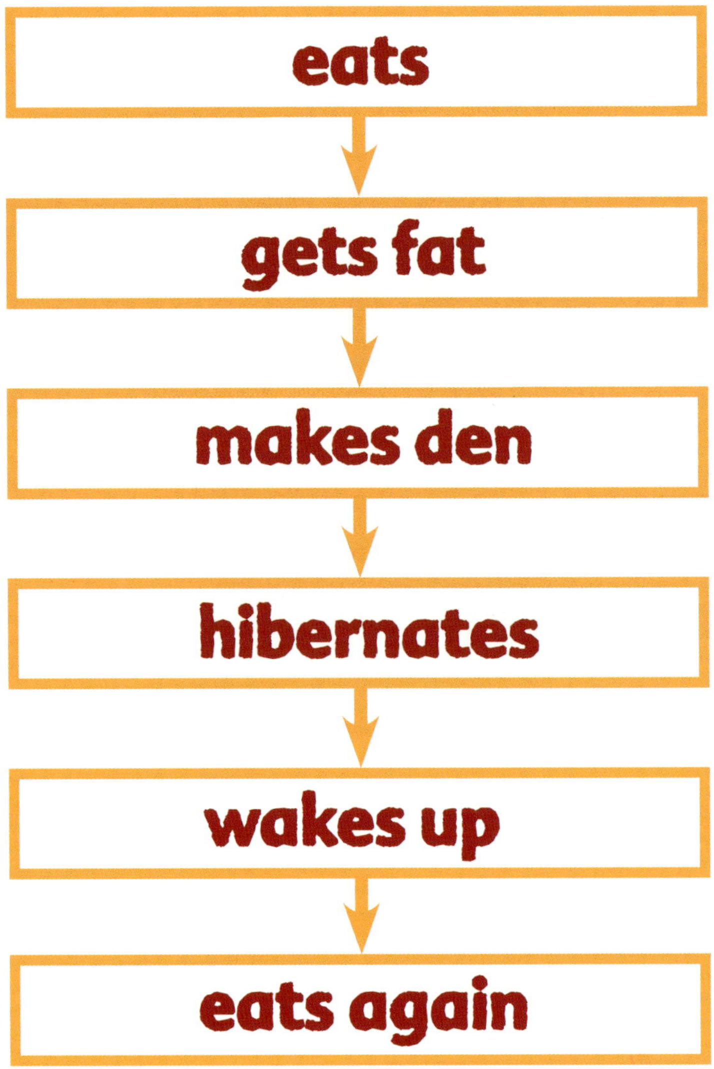

Words to Know

cave

cubs

den

Index